M000084591

DIVING DOLPHINS

by Laura Hamilton Waxman

Pull Ahead Books

⌐ Lerner Publications Company • Minneapolis

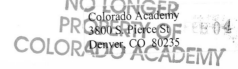

This book is available in two editions:
Library binding by Lerner Publications Company, a division of Lerner Publishing Group
Soft cover by First Avenue Editions, an imprint of Lerner Publishing Group
241 First Avenue North
Minneapolis, MN 55401

Website address: www.lernerbooks.com

Words in *italic* type are explained in a glossary on page 30.

Library of Congress Cataloging-in-Publication Data

Waxman, Laura Hamilton.
    Diving dolphins / by Laura Hamilton Waxman.
        p.   cm. — (Pull ahead books)
    Summary: Describes physical characteristics of
dolphins, how they swim, how they breathe, what they
eat, and how they raise their young.
        ISBN 0–8225–0684–X (lib. bdg. : alk. paper)
        ISBN 0–8225–0964–4 (pbk. : alk. paper)
        1. Dolphins—Juvenile literature. [1. Dolphins.]
    I. Title. II. Series.
    QL737.C432 W39   2003
    599.53—dc21   2001006141

Manufactured in the United States of America
1 2 3 4 5 6 — JR — 08 07 06 05 04 03

Look!
An animal is diving into the water.

Is it a big fish?

No! This animal is a dolphin.

Most dolphins live in the ocean.

Other dolphins live in rivers.

Where do you live?

A dolphin's body is made for moving through the water.

Smooth skin helps a dolphin glide easily.

A strong tail pushes the dolphin through the water.

How many dolphin tails do you see here?

Two *flippers* help a dolphin steer.

One flipper is on each side of the dolphin's body.

A *fin* helps a dolphin balance
as it swims.

The fin sticks up from
the dolphin's back.

Dolphins can swim much faster
than humans can.

Sometimes dolphins leap
through the air as they swim.

Dolphins can dive deep
under the water, too.

Dolphins can stay underwater
for a long time.

But they must breathe air.
How does a dolphin breathe?

A dolphin sticks its head
out of the water to breathe.

The dolphin blows air out of a hole called a *blowhole*.

Then the dolphin breathes air
into its lungs through its blowhole.

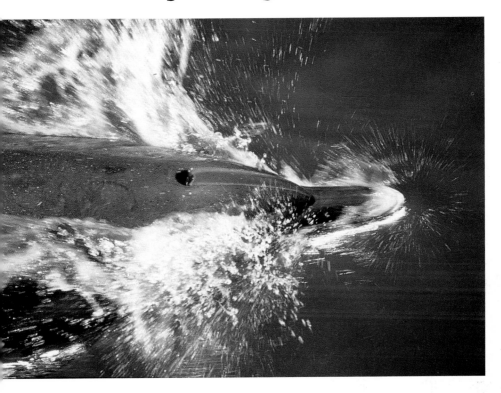

This dolphin is breathing
while it swims.

Most dolphins swim together
in *schools.*

A school is a group of dolphins.

The dolphins in a school
play together.

What else does a school of dolphins
do together?

A school of dolphins
looks for food together.

Dolphins are *predators*.

Predators are animals that hunt
and eat other animals.

Dolphins eat fish and other small sea animals.

This dolphin is eating an octopus.

Dolphins use their sharp teeth
to catch and eat food.

This baby dolphin is eating.
But it is not eating a fish.

The baby dolphin is *nursing*.
It is drinking milk from its mother.

Dolphins are *mammals.*

Mammals are animals that make milk to feed their young.

A baby dolphin is called a *calf*.

A calf stays close to its mother
for more than one year.

The calf also stays near the other dolphins in its school.

These dolphins help the mother take care of her calf.

The calf learns to play and hunt.

It is growing up.

Soon it will be a big, diving dolphin!

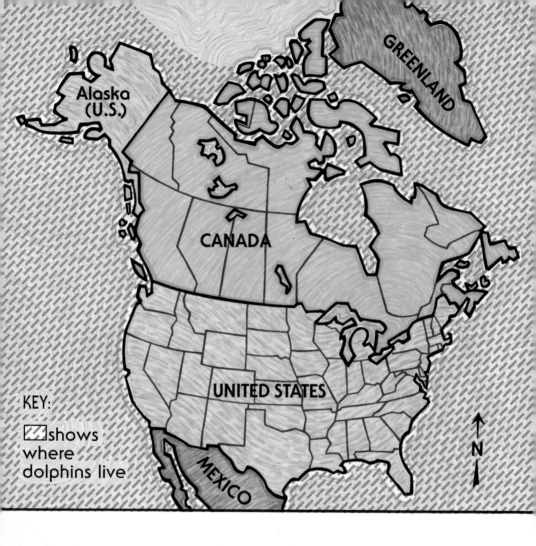

KEY:
⬚ shows where dolphins live

Find your state or province on this map.
Do dolphins live near you?

Parts of a Dolphin's Body

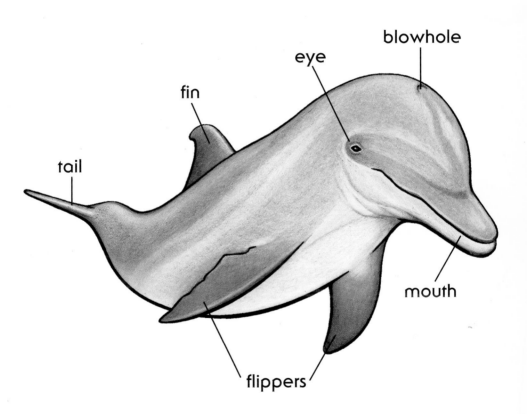

blowhole

eye

fin

tail

mouth

flippers

Glossary

blowhole: the hole through which a dolphin breathes

calf: a baby dolphin

fin: the flat part that sticks up from a dolphin's back.
The fin helps the dolphin to balance as it swims.

flippers: two flat parts that stick out from the sides of a
dolphin's body. Flippers help a dolphin to steer
through the water.

mammals: animals that make milk to feed their
young

nursing: drinking mother's milk

predators: animals that hunt and eat other animals

schools: groups of dolphins

Hunt and Find

- a dolphin **breathing** on pages 5, 9, 13, 14–15

- a dolphin **calf** on pages 22–26

- a dolphin **catching food** on pages 18–20

- dolphins **leaping** out of the water on pages 3, 10, 17, 26, 27

- a **school** of dolphins on pages 16–17, 25

- a dolphin's **teeth** on pages 6, 21

About the Author

Laura Hamilton Waxman grew up in Saint Louis, Missouri. She saw dolphins for the first time on a childhood trip to North Carolina and quickly fell in love with the sleek, fun-loving creatures. Laura currently lives in Minneapolis, Minnesota, where she works as a children's book author and editor.

Photo Acknowledgments

The photographs in this book are reproduced with the permission of: © Tim Davis/Photo Researchers, Inc., front cover, pp. 23, 24, 25; © Masa Ushioda/Seapics.com, p. 3; © Ingrid Visser/Seapics.com, pp. 4, 12; © Leonide Principe/Photo Researchers, Inc., p. 5; © Bob Cranston, pp. 6, 11; © Doug Perrine/Seapics.com, pp. 7, 19, 21, 22; © James D. Watt/Seapics.com, p. 8; © F. Stuart Westmorland/Photo Researchers, Inc., pp. 9, 27; © Michael S. Nolan/Wildlife Images/Tom Stack and Associates, p. 10; © Brian Parker/Tom Stack & Associates, pp. 13, 31; © Tom Stack/Tom Stack and Associates, p. 14; © Robert Pitman/Seapics.com, p. 15; © Phillip Colla/Seapics.com, p. 16; © Michael S. Nolan/Seapics.com, pp. 17, 26; © Roland Seitre/Seapics.com, p. 18; © Dan Burton/Seapics.com, p. 20.